GET CROWNED!

Sparking a Heaven on Earth Transformation

THERESA MCMORROW JORDAN, M.A.

Get Crowned!
Copyright © 2021 by Theresa McMorrow Jordan, M.A.
668 Granite Ln.
Fairfield, CA 94534
Your Phone Number (423)408-4109
Your Email Address (theresa.mj@hotmail.com)
Your Website Address
(www.HeavenonEarthTransformation.com)

All rights reserved. No part of this publication may be reproduced, distributed, or transmitted in any form or by any means, including photocopying, recording, or other electronic or mechanical methods, without the prior written permission of the author, except in the case of brief quotations embodied in critical reviews and certain other non-commercial uses permitted by copyright law.

Limits of Liability and Disclaimer of Warranty
The author and publisher shall not be liable for your misuse of this material. This book is strictly for informational and educational purposes.

Warning – Disclaimer
The purpose of this book is to educate and entertain. The author and/or publisher do not guarantee that anyone following these techniques, suggestions, tips, ideas, or strategies will become successful. The author and/or publisher shall have neither liability nor responsibility to anyone with respect to any loss or damage caused, or alleged to be caused, directly or indirectly by the information contained in this book.

ISBN
978-1-954932-23-4 (Paperback)
978-1-954932-22-7 (eBook)

Theresa McMorrow Jordan, M.A.
Former Catholic Nun, Mother of Two Sons, Champion of Greatness in Individuals, Young or Old, Families, Communities, Employees, Businesses, Churches And Schools Lover of Souls, Lover of God and all His Created Universe

Dedication

To my two sons, Jeffrey and Seth, even the amazing
accomplishment of this book pales in comparison
to the moment I first laid eyes on you!
May, you, too, receive this call with open arms and
go forward and create your most prosperous life, with
your crown in view and your souls fully activated!
I love you all the way to Heaven and back!

Table of Contents

Dedication v
Acknowledgement 1
Forward 3
Perspective 5
Introduction... 7
Special Promise 9
"I want you close." 11
"Begin with the end in mind" 17
The Vision and The Crown 23
A special Activation of The SOUL 31
The Soul-powered Heaven on Earth Revolution 37
HEAVEN on EARTH Transformation Mission 45
Living with THE CROWN in mind 67
CROWN-based Communities... 69
CROWN-based Business Partners 71
Final Thoughts 73

Acknowledgement

Where do I begin? I have been so blessed from birth to have been surrounded by everyone and everything I needed – although I haven't always had the eyes to see it that way. This book is my special "take" on the world, or on the ultimate purpose we have as human beings, but not meant to be comprehensive by any means. If I tried to list all who influenced my philosophy and choices taken, I would have to start with my beautifully loving parents, Mike and Kathleen, my brothers: Michael, Jamie †, Joseph, Lawrence, Sean, Anthony, and Stephen. My Aunt Anne and her girls, my cousins, Jane, Jackie and Catherine. My dearest childhood friends, Margie, Sue, Michelle, Kathy Brahaney, The Sisters Devoted to the Sacred heart of Jesus, **JESUS, who captured my heart at 7 years of age,** my cousin, Father Willie Dever, My only husband, Jerry Glenn Jordan, my beautiful sons, Jeffrey and Seth. And the powerful cover of intercessors that God has continued over me that I could not begin to list……since I left the convent. Pastor Fairbanks, Pastor Mike Murdoch, Sid Roth, and those who influenced me through their songs, Mercy Me, Chris Tomlin, and their writings, Teresa of Avila, Therese Lisieux, Victor Frankel, Julia Cameron, Billye Brim, Napoleon Hill, Anthony Robbins, Jim Rohn, Louise Hay, Loral Langemeier,

Wayne Dyer, Abraham (Esther Hicks) and most recently, Mel Robbins. The authors of all of the books I have read, numerous Ted talks and You Tube videos, not to mention the 1,000's of one on one conversations I have had with so many throughout my journey. All of you who have been in my life, for a moment, a month, for years, you have all played a part of sculpting me – and at times, breaking my heart, so that I could love from a deeper place with deeper understanding and perspective. You took me into your heart, and walked by my side, near and far, thank you. You touched me in profound ways – and you played a part in this most loving work. It is my hope that it inspires you, encourages you, kicks you into gear so that you jump back into your life and make something extra special out of ToDAY, and out of the remainder of your days. XXXOOO

Forward

You know when God chooses you to do something; you just may as well do it because He isn't going to let you rest! Yes, I went through all of the excuses why I wasn't the right person to bring such an important message to the world and He caused me to see Wayne Dyer live on PBS presenting his new book, Excuses Be Gone!

I tried to remind Him that most of the people He would really like to get this message across to, find me too intense, too outside of the box! He then chose to use one of my own favorite responses against me, "and your point is"?

I asked Him why He didn't assign this to someone famous, well-respected, well-known, like the Pope, or OPRAH, or the Dalai Lama; they have huge captive audiences already and whatever they say is like Gospel before ever a word is spoken?

And so, clearly understanding that I am by far, not properly positioned in any way to be the channel for this most important Last call, I whole-heartedly present it to you, standing in the BOLD KNOWLEDGE of this being a God-given assignment!

For those of you who know me personally you can probably also imagine me madly designing CROWNS so that people can wear them and plaster them everywhere as they "Get the Call!" and as you read the message of the book, you will soon realize that my mind is going a million miles an hour with ideas of how to support the birthing of this new level of consciousness and heavenliness!

This is a serious Last Call, but as only God can do, it is a last call filled with an infinite number of incredible possibilities of which I simply paint a high-level sketch of the living vision board.

From this book, the real mission work will begin—and I look forward to working on this together with you in some capacity.

Thank you and God's choicest blessings,

Theresa McMorrow Jordan, M.A.

Perspective

This Book is a Special Event in my life, as you can well imagine. More importantly, I believe it is one of several EVENTS that God is choosing to use to shift the focus of humanity and communicate His Heart and Vision for the 2020 decade. I am just bursting at the seams of my soul to get the message of this book out and to the ends of the Earth!

    Perhaps a recent example will make a Global shift in humanity seem more credible. Sometimes reflecting on recent events best demonstrates the possibility of such BIG Thoughts. For example, one core message of my book is that God wants to shift our distant relationship to Him to a soulmate relationship with Him. Here is an example of how easy it is today to shift all of humanity through one event.

    Recently we saw such a shift in a relationship of humanity; we witnessed the wedding of a young couple, Harry and Meghan. A year or so ago, they were featured here and there in the gossip magazines and in the media; now, since their media-blitzed wedding, millions of people, can now recognize them if they saw them in a coffee shop. Now, Harry and Meghan, are their Duke and Duchess of Sussex, to those living in the UK, and now the couple will have many shout out to them, wherever they go, asking for a smile, a photo or an autograph. Their close and personal friends and acquaintances might be expecting to be included in all the many posh and exclusive parties they will now be invited to attend.

God, your creator is looking for such a shift in your relationship to Him and His relationship to all of humanity. I hope that by sharing the incredible ideas He has opened my mind to understand, you, too, will be inspired to press into Him close and enjoy the same soulmate relationship as I do. He promises, this closer relationship with Him will bring much more to you than a smile, an autograph or a photo with the Duke and Duchess.

I sincerely hope that the contents of this book, may in some small but compelling way, expedite that shift, lead you to a whole new life of soul-exploration and Self[10]-realization, and to genuine experiences of Heaven on Earth in all aspects of your life. I know this is the start of an adventure and I hope you will be a part of this amazing dream for the 2020 decade.

I truly desire that this is just the beginning of a very special friendship.

Theresa McMorrow Jordan, M.A.

Introduction

So, in this Book I reveal the heart of God for this time, as He has revealed it to me; it is not meant to be comprehensive, for I am only one soul. If you are still wondering why He would choose me to reveal this, don't worry, I have asked Him that question many times myself. I do have to say, I have enjoyed a close and personal relationship with God my whole life; I am not a Saint by any stretch of the imagination. I just think that He stole my heart all the way back when I was 7 years old preparing for my First Holy Communion.

More than anything, He knows He takes my breath away, and perhaps that is why He wants you to hear it through me.

1) God, as I said, wants a close, soul to soul, 24/7 mindful of His loving presence, relationship with you.
2) In this ERA --- I was inspired to call this final ERA, a SOUL Revolution – He wants you to really KNOW Him; He wants you and all of humanity to come to understand the most important and as yet underutilized part of His design of us, as human beings, our SOUL.

3) He wants you to know that with this new breakthrough knowledge and mastery of the utilization of our SOUL's incredible powers, we have an opportunity to see lots of HEAVEN on EARTH by the end of this decade.
4) He wants the individual soul and the World of souls to understand that without this shift in humanity…. To the HIGHEST design of ourselves, soul-led, not body-led, a very different outcome could prevail. The Good News is that those who make the shift, will not suffer the Day of Destruction no matter what!
5) He wants us to begin with the end in mind and I will share with you THE CROWN He will place on your head and how He wants you to keep that special encounter forefront in your mind throughout these years to 2020 and beyond.
6) He wants us to learn HIS WAYS that are inclusive, elevating, compelling, Life-giving, Ever-flowing, non-coercive, slow to anger, rich in mercy, championing, and LOVING!
7) Lastly, this shift, will bring in a LIFE existence not yet even imagined…. WONDER full in every way possible!

This my dear friend, is just a sharing of the core vision; You are, by the purchase of this book, being given an opportunity to play a special role in sharing its content, promoting its content, and or being a part of designing and building Crown-based businesses and Crown-based communities…or simply usher in a little bit of Heaven into your world.

Introduction

So, in this Book I reveal the heart of God for this time, as He has revealed it to me; it is not meant to be comprehensive, for I am only one soul. If you are still wondering why He would choose me to reveal this, don't worry, I have asked Him that question many times myself. I do have to say, I have enjoyed a close and personal relationship with God my whole life; I am not a Saint by any stretch of the imagination. I just think that He stole my heart all the way back when I was 7 years old preparing for my First Holy Communion.

More than anything, He knows He takes my breath away, and perhaps that is why He wants you to hear it through me.

1) God, as I said, wants a close, soul to soul, 24/7 mindful of His loving presence, relationship with you.
2) In this ERA --- I was inspired to call this final ERA, a SOUL Revolution – He wants you to really KNOW Him; He wants you and all of humanity to come to understand the most important and as yet underutilized part of His design of us, as human beings, our SOUL.

3) He wants you to know that with this new breakthrough knowledge and mastery of the utilization of our SOUL's incredible powers, we have an opportunity to see lots of HEAVEN on EARTH by the end of this decade.
4) He wants the individual soul and the World of souls to understand that without this shift in humanity…. To the HIGHEST design of ourselves, soul-led, not body-led, a very different outcome could prevail. The Good News is that those who make the shift, will not suffer the Day of Destruction no matter what!
5) He wants us to begin with the end in mind and I will share with you THE CROWN He will place on your head and how He wants you to keep that special encounter forefront in your mind throughout these years to 2020 and beyond.
6) He wants us to learn HIS WAYS that are inclusive, elevating, compelling, Life-giving, Ever-flowing, non-coercive, slow to anger, rich in mercy, championing, and LOVING!
7) Lastly, this shift, will bring in a LIFE existence not yet even imagined…. WONDER full in every way possible!

This my dear friend, is just a sharing of the core vision; You are, by the purchase of this book, being given an opportunity to play a special role in sharing its content, promoting its content, and or being a part of designing and building Crown-based businesses and Crown-based communities…or simply usher in a little bit of Heaven into your world.

Special Promise

You know you are involved in a move of God when almost everything currently existing is included in the move forward, without disrupting or requiring that souls abandon their core beliefs. God has an amazing way of taking us where we currently are and lifting us up--- His methods are painless… if you really look closely at any move of God, it is often the human instrument that stepped in and made a mess of things….. I am trying very hard in this assignment not to get into His way:

- Of calling you ever more deeply into His companionship
- by inspiring you to consider this expose` on your soul and The Crown and how it could possibly be the rocket into your next level of greatness
- And by inviting you to join, on your own terms, this special Heaven on Earth project.

Just for purchasing my book I would like to give you a little sign of my appreciation; just go to my website, <u>www.heavenonearthtransformation.com</u> to download this gift.

"I want you close."
~God

You would like your life journey to be a little more like Heaven, wouldn't you? You would love to be a part of an era where healing, loving, prosperous communities sprung into being without war? What about an era where discoveries were made that reversed aging, where sickness and hunger were a thing of the past? Where excellence gave way to Excellence with the realization that together, not by demanding the abandonment of culture, religious beliefs or understanding, not through dictatorship or control, but through our common understanding of our souls? Where there is a Soul, there is a special agent of God, The Creator, inscribed with a particular mission/assignment in the universe.

    A special secret: God wants you close. He doesn't want you to come close, once you straighten out your life, once you go to confession, once you go back to Church; he wants you to come to Him, soul to soul, He is near, right here, right now! You are always in His Presence; we have only to become mindful of that fact, and the JOY of the knowledge of the reality of His loving presence, like a breath of fresh spring air, will rush in, to renew your spirit! He knows all about every detail of your life; and He still loves you, as the bedtime story goes, all the way to the moon and back! Why? Because He watched you be knit in your mother's womb. Even if your Mother or Father abandoned you, He has never abandoned you. He went way out of His way to prove that you are a unique and independent thought and creation of His; by your fingerprints, your retina, your very DNA. Everything in the universe began as a thought, an idea in the mind of God. You were a thought in God's mind before you grew in your Mother's womb and entered into this world. He wants you to know that you were beautifully and wonderfully made by Him!

To those of you well-versed in the Scriptures you will recall the one sin Jesus was pretty adamant about...... Jesus said that to him/her who does anything to lead a soul astray or make coming to God complicated or near impossible, that it would be better for them to have a millstone wrapped around their neck and be thrown into the sea! The reason is because God hates wedges put between a soul and Him, especially by Religious Leaders/Ministers who either violate a soul directly or put ridiculous obstacles to God through their man-made controls. We need to gain a God Perspective on some of our long-held beliefs and practices. I look forward to live discussions with you at a later date in an open webinar format. Bottom line is God wants us all close to Him in our daily lives.

What if I told you that God is not requiring you to be a Buddhist, a Christian, a Catholic, a Baptist, Muslim, a Jehovah's Witness, Non-Denominational, New Age, or otherwise, in order to gain access to Him and receive this knowledge of His design of humanity. To those of us who have been given the special grace of knowing God's greatest Love Story of humanity, Jesus, you, will recall his instruction to his disciples when they came to him complaining that someone "outside" of their group was healing. He told them not to worry, you will know them by their fruits, if they are true disciples or not. Somehow, we have misunderstood the fact that it is God who draws all souls to Himself. Even as a Catholic nun it was never my aim to make more Catholics, it was always my clear intention to do all I could to lead them to an Encounter with God. I understood that without a real experience of the presence of God, no amount of Catechism would turn a heart and soul toward loving God. I was completely dedicated to giving them as much knowledge of God, through music and presentations, from the rich vault of spiritual teachings of the Catholic Church so that they could walk out their lives close to God, confirmed in His Highest Call and committed to building strong relationships, families and communities in the Church and in the World.

I am not suggesting that we leave the Churches or Religions we are in; rather, He opened my heart and mind to understand that He doesn't prefer one over the other. In fact He uses them all to draw all of humanity, soul by soul into the fullness of His presence. I will not go into detail my thesis on why everyone on the Earth is not Christian by now; suffice it to say, God doesn't need that to be the case to move forward His wonderful Plan for us!

Trust me, as a practicing Catholic and a former nun, it took me by surprise, when He conveyed this fact to me. One morning, when I was in prayer in my living room, trying to prepare an outreach as a Catholic, into the Bible belt community I was living, this question emerged: "You do know that when you die, I am not going to ask you if you were Catholic?" That question He raised in my heart in that manner completely burned away all of my fears about being a Catholic trying to lead community-building activities. I firmly believe because **I** didn't have it as an issue, it became a moot issue in time. I approached my work like Paul did to the Colossians, Philippians, The Hebrews, and Corinthians, and I to the Baptists, the Assembly of Gods, the Methodists, the Ruritanian, Pentecostals, and Non-Denominationalists, etc. I absolutely fell in love with all of them; their love of God and service to the community was exceptional. They found it impossible, in time, though not all, to resist my genuine, passionate and loving intention to collaborate and make our common vision for Community show up where all could see and enjoy! (*And by the way, if the Colossians, Corinthians, Philippians, Ephesians, all lived in the same community, they may not have gotten along very well either – just saying,,,*)

So, God wants you close, and all I can say is, you know what to do to remove any barriers to a quality relationship with God, just do it! If you get stuck, ask yourself is there anyone you look up to that has a close relationship with God and call them. If you hit a wall, you are welcome to contact me and I will help you.

I believe, like many others before me, that God has provided a portal to His heart in your life, and if that is the Catholic Church, the Buddhist temple, the Jewish Temple, a Muslim mosque, a Science of the Mind Center, or whatever House of Worship, or even the memory of your grandmother's Faith in God, if you are not a "Church-goer… start there and rediscover why He gave you that portal. He is leading all souls to Himself. Your portal should be all about strengthening your connection to God, teaching you how to enter and walk in His presence, inspiring you to live your highest possible life. You can never go wrong when you seek out the TRUTH about Him, and be the best Christian, Buddhist, Muslim, Catholic, New Age, Human being… but don't be surprised if when you seek Him, I mean really seek Him, He may call you up and out of where you are in this process— Do not be afraid— He wants you to know Him personally—and depending on Your call to action, in this ERA, God may need you somewhere else to do your special call!

"Begin with the end in mind"
~Stephen Covey

I believe most people have heard this wisdom shared by Stephen Covey, author of many books, and this particular quote is from 12 Habits of Highly Effective People. What it means, to refresh your memory, is if you want to achieve anything in your life, begin with a visual of you accomplishing it. Tony Robbins would say, create a full blown video experience in your mind, sitting behind the wheel of that red hot corvette; drive the car in your imagination, with the top down, along Pacific Coast Highway on a perfect California day. You don't have to exactly know how you are ever going to afford that Red Corvette, but it is amazing how, once you create that LIVE 3 D picture (some even go and test drive one) it sets up a whole new energy that allows you to come up with some creative new ways to generate income and make that Red Corvette a reality in no time! I can tell you that this practice works, on highly valued "Things", to Personal achievement of Higher Education, a promotion, a relationship.

God pressed on my heart that He wants us to put at the top priority of our LISTS, the moment in the future where we will GET Crowned by Him. At the end of this journey, we will all meet Him face to face, soul to soul. He wants us to imagine that moment, how do we want it to go. Do we want to arrive to that moment like the guy in the Parable of the Talents, who felt that because His Master only gave him a few talents he better bury them so he wouldn't lose the few he was given. He reasoned that at least when His Master would return, he would have *something* to show. God wants you to understand, because this man chose to bury his talents he missed out on the quality of life God had in mind for him and those around him were cheated too because he lived a half-life!

There was another compelling story Jesus told about a rich man Lazarus that was selfish and was in no way moved by the needs of others. He even had a good and faithful servant who needed his help, but Lazarus refused to help him. It was told that Lazarus spent his whole life "all about him", rejecting all of the invitations by God to change and so when he passed from this life he went to the place of His choosing.... Hell, where He didn't have to share with anyone.... And then Lazarus' servant died and went to Heaven where he enjoyed the full banquet. Lazarus begged from hell that he be allowed to go back and visit his brothers and tell them the Truth about Life. God denied his request, saying essentially that they would not receive any additional messages; God had sent prophet after prophet to them and yet they refused to listen.

This book is the sharing of a private revelation of God and you don't have to believe it. But I cannot rest until I share it with you. God wants you to put THE CROWN, the moment you will meet Him face to face in the forefront of your mind's eye, as you walk through the remainder of your days. It is his desire that THE CROWN will serve to remind you both of His deep abiding Love for you and of His call to come to know your Soul and its powers; study and incorporate its amazing powers into your day, and watch what you are able to achieve going forward.

God has already revealed in the scriptures that He gives out Crowns in some sort of really special way, in Heaven---and for some reason He has chosen me to convey this special request of His. I will share in the next chapter how He revealed this to me.

So, to get you going on the visualization of your crown, it is important to take a few moments to consider your life thus far. If it is difficult for you to consider your accomplishments think of what makes you proud of the other people in your life. If you are a parent, consider all the moments in your child's life that made you beam with pure JOY! Imagine, this is how God, your Creator gazes upon you, His child! Can you see a few GEMS on your crown yet?

"That moment, when you will finally meet your Creator, face to face, makes every moment in this life matter!"

The Vision and The Crown

Have you ever been compelled to do something in your life? Have you ever had something happen to you that changed your life and then it was as if an assignment came from deep inside of you? Have you ever received A Call to action that no matter how much you tried to drown it out, it still kept nagging at you to get it done? Well that is why I am forsaking all thoughts of how this will be received or what will others think of me. Something happened that so changed my life and my perspective on my life; and God will not let me rest until I share this amazing experience with you. By the way, when I was a nun in the convent, I never had a vision from God... believe me as a young religious, I was fervently begging God to show His heart to me!

This is how the vision took place:

It was not unusual at all that I would share one of my original songs and a testimony at my husband's family's Baptist Church; they made me, as the only Catholic most of them had ever actually met, feel welcomed and loved. I had felt the presence of the Holy Spirit and their strong Faith and Love of Jesus since the first time we met!

This particular morning I was so moved to a stream of unending tears.... Like a cleansing pool of water accompanied by a voice, though not audible with my ears that said: "I have a fierce enemy who attacked you with doubt about your vocation to be a nun, until you left; he did so for had you stayed, you would have done a lot of good".

How do I communicate to you the power of this Grace. I had prayed to hear directly from God that leaving the convent was the right decision; for in my heart of hearts, being a nun was my true vocation. I made a forever commitment to God; to be forever His, alone; to serve Him and to lead souls to Him. Yes, the Catholic Bishop had officially released me from those vows I had made to God, publicly; but I had always longed to hear it from God, himself.

To add to this question about God being disappointed with me, 90 days after I left the convent, I was raped. As a nun, I had worked in high crime zones at night and never came close to any danger.... This experience made me feel like my decision to leave the convent removed a covering of protection from me.... that I was "on my own!" It was the practice of that order to have no further contact with you if you chose to leave...so in fact, I was on my own; and I mostly felt like a fish out of water.

So, to have God, all these years later, reach into my heart, my soul, and personally tell me that He is not upset at me; that His love has not diminished and that He is not holding me to that vow........ was liberating to say the least. This was the first sense of PEACE I had received since leaving the convent so many years before......

It was confusing to me as well, for I did not understand, why now, so many years later, would you visit me with this healing to the soul of my soul message? And He proceeded to open my mind to understand this and so much more. One very significant event happened at that very time; I found out that Sr. Ida Peterfy, the foundress of that order of nuns, had died. I was very close to her and loved her deeply.

He explained that the words I received at the Baptist Church were the same words that Sister Ida received, and she was then able to forgive me… and I was given the added grace of forgiveness on this side. I came to understand that Sister Ida had already seen in me the potential to be a future leader in the order she had founded; a person she could hand the baton to. When I chose to leave, she thought that I had just abandoned my vocation, and had done so casually. Once she understood that I was targeted by the enemy of God, she completely forgave me.

As a footnote, He revealed to me that unforgiveness is the most toxic behavior of all human behaviors, and causes the highest level of pain and suffering in this life. When we forgive on this side, without all of the facts, special and abundant graces are showered upon all involved. It is unnecessary to go directly to the person; as soon as you release someone in your heart they are released. Take a few moments to consider individuals you may be carrying in unforgiveness or individuals you have harmed and write down a few thoughts taking it to the Lord, that He may help you forgive or find a way to make amends….. know that I have already been praying for you to take this step.

_____
_____
_____
_____
_____
_____
_____
_____

The Lord opened my mind in the next couple of weeks to understand many things about our passing from this life to the next and how He hopes with this new understanding, souls would have burdens lifted from them and become free to bring their highest lives into being. How He longs that we would enjoy living this gift of Life, at the highest level of His design—mind, body and soul!

Perhaps you are carrying around unanswered questions of God, about decisions you have made or actions you have taken or didn't take that altered your life path significantly. I will pray right now, this second, that God will convey to you the same deep Peace in your soul about your past, so that you can be fully present in His call NOW! I have learned that the call on our lives never changes it just morphs! Perhaps a few questions are emerging inside of your heart.... Here are a few lines reserved for you to bring those questions of God to the surface – He wants you to come to Him with your questions....

_____
_____
_____
_____
_____
_____
_____
_____
_____
_____
_____

He also revealed to me, over a period of about a month the Heaven orientation process, to put it into Human Resources terms. When we pass, from this life to the next, an angel meets us and spends "time with us" showing little bits and pieces of our lives played back on something that appeared like the mirrored tiles of the disco ball (that is the best way for me to describe). This time you get to see those moments with all the facts, from God's perspective, and with all the facts, you are easily able to forgive and are systematically healed from all the pain and suffering of your life on Earth. It is like a bath of soul-level healing and restoration to our Highest self.

Next, God opened my eyes to understand that more of His angels will come with this most beautiful crown, covered in jewels; and pointing at each gem, bring to your full recollection the corresponding sweet act of love, mercy, kindness, generosity, sacrifice, goodness you did while living your life on Earth. Imagine, God, like a proud Papa, creates this beautiful crown of jewels that mirrors all that was good about you during your life on Earth! He understands, by designing you with a free will, you could choose not to LOVE, Forgive, Share, Multiply Returns on the Gifts that He gave you. Every time you choose to LOVE, it melts His Heart and He says, That's My Boy! Or That's My Girl!

(So you mean God has not spent our whole lives on this planet, recounting all of our sins and failings, but rather collecting and categorizing into gems, all of the love and kindness and courage we have demonstrated throughout our life on Earth?) Yes!!! Then why are **we** focusing on all of our sins and failings instead of following a TO LOVE and To LIVE Fully list every day?

I, myself, was weeping at this Truth; just to realize that God, my Creator, is so invested in each of us, His creations; He is such a champion and lover of us all!

Next, He revealed that we will be clothed and crowned by the angels and led into the breath-taking presence of God. What do you think that moment will be like for you? I encourage you to pause and reflect on what that moment is going to be like.

Would you agree, that moment, when you will finally meet your Creator, face to face, is the only moment that really matters in your whole life? Truly, that moment, makes every moment in life matter!!!

A special Activation of The SOUL

To help you really take this thought deeper, I strongly recommend that you go to YOU Tube and listen to these two songs which were playing on Christian radio around the time God gave me this vision; songs like these are special Graces of God. The two songs are: "I Can Only Imagine" by Mercy Me and " We Fall Down, We Lay Our Crowns, at the feet of Jesus", by Chris Tomlin….. taking a few moments will really help you create a fully developed picture in your mind of this moment and help the sacredness, the goosebump experience of His JOY-filled presence resound in your soul, (Go out to You Tube and play these songs right now…. I have prayed that to those who do, they will receive a special sense of God's presence; an affirmation that what I am sharing here is TRUTH) I hope that you will consider purchasing these songs to add to your library and promote the tremendous talent of these artists.

How are you feeling about this vision I received? Is it shifting anything inside of your mind, heart and/or soul? I, myself, was stopped in my tracks by this vision…. All I could think about was now that I "get it" I want my crown to be full of jewels. Above all my personal dreams and aspirations, I want to be a JOY to my creator, Father, God…. At the end of my life, I want to run like a child into His arms and hear him say, "Well done, my child; you brought me great JOY and consolation throughout your whole life journey! And then I thought perhaps, upon entering His presence, a great AWE would fill me up, and I would fall down on my knees and lay down my crown at His feet, covered with His sweetest, most loving presence. This Vision and new understanding of God's utmost desire for me caused me to become profoundly aware, even after years in the convent, that I had no idea, no real depth of comprehension of who God is, the greatness of His greatness, nor did I fully grasp the meaning of this moment.... I knew with a knowledge as if imprinted on every cell in my body, that God, my Creator, loved me into being and is entirely committed to championing me into my highest being!!! At that moment, when I knelt before my most loving Creator God, I was overcome by the most compelling desire to love more deeply and make a proper return to the Lord for all the gifts and talents He has given me.... I just wanted to run to the streets and in fact to the ends of the Earth and tell everyone what the LORD had opened the eyes of my soul to see, so that they, too, could both enjoy this life as is God's design and not waste it!!! It was truly a Heaven on Earth moment for me!

To say the least, I was a weeping mess surrounded by the loving presence of God! That night I tossed and turned and hardly slept at all; I arose in the morning with a great sadness that my crown was empty of jewels... that I hadn't done anything yet.... To which God in His sweetness, replied in the depth of my soul, "Look, here in the center of your crown is a most beautiful diadem, for you gave me your youth!" I am crying just recalling that moment, for a moment like this with God is always in the NOW..... can always be revisited in the present.... Only God, Himself, could have said that to me; no one else would know just what to say to reassure me.... Not superficially but to the deepest recesses of my heart!

Now it is your turn to take a moment and tell God, your Creator whatever comes to your mind, your heart, your soul. I have left some lines for you to write down any thoughts that come to your mind about your Crown and about this revelation.

_____

_____

_____

_____

_____

_____

_____

_____

_____

_____

_____

_____

_____

_____

_____

_____

_____

_____

_____

"God made us with free will and He wants us to know that by pursuing the latest knowledge and utilization of our SOUL's incredible powers, we have an opportunity to see HEAVEN on EARTH by the end of this decade."

The Soul-powered Heaven on Earth Revolution

You do recognize that we live in an age of complexity and have gone through a couple of decades of massive core infrastructure change to our connections with one another and with what is going on locally and all around the world. We have exponentially way more information to wade through on a daily basis, then any past generation. It is no wonder that most fail to make the time to BE STILL and KNOW God, never mind navigate all the dysfunctional aspects of their particular culture/religion/government/family/community that is keeping you from living your highest life as an individual. What do I mean by that?

As I have shared, God wants us to live close, mindfully one with Him throughout this Life. He is wanting to clearly state that the distance you and I are experiencing in our relationship with Him has been caused by a number of factors, many that simply have to do with the time in which we live and others have to do with a distortion of His Word and/or a limited understanding of His true intentions.

There are 3 adjustments required to live out the remainder of your life in the fullest design of your humanity, mind, body and soul.

1) You must carve out time to be alone, just you and God, at least 3 short uninterrupted times a day; first thing in the morning, some point mid-day, and at the very end of your day.
2) You must remove all of the wedges between you and God and
3) You must study everything you can that is being written on the power of the mind and soul right now; continuously add levels of mastery to your gifts and talents and learn how to build joint ventures and collaborations with others. If you want to enjoy a Heaven on Earth existence you must learn to operate more and more from your SOUL, your center of Excellence.

So the first adjustment required to enjoy a rapid deployment of the ever flowing Life energy of your soul, is to make time in your day, at the beginning, the middle and the end of your day to mindfully, consciously plug in, soul to soul with God, your Creator, and endless source of Life flow. You may already have a favorite way to do this, reading the scriptures; reading the Words of the Psalms, 8, 91, 15 out loud to God is a great place to start. My favorite psalm, and one in which I have written many songs around is Psalm 23, The Lord is My Shepherd.

God, like ourselves, absolutely loves to be praised and to hear how much we love Him. I really think we have no clue the unbelievable power we have been given by God, the power to freely choose to Love Him or not; to be in a relationship, or not. Did you know that God created the covenant of Marriage? He designed it to be a LIVING symbol of His Covenant to faithfully Love Us and Our Covenant to faithfully Love Him. Well, I guess you can see by our statistics, we have a ways to go in our development to restore Marriage and the Vows of Marriage to His beautiful original design. I believe that this gap is that we are trying to live out our covenants without utilizing the highest power of our beings, our soul.

Our particular Free Will power as humans is not in His design of the Angels…. The movie, "The City of Angels", captures and portrays some of the extraordinary components in God's design of us as humans. Choosing to acknowledge God and not ourselves as The Creator, and seeking to live aligned with His highest design of us, ushers in a flow of GRACE that is unending and abiding and loving.

The second action, remove any and all wedges that exist between you and God and the desire to study, I mean really dig in and investigate to understand. You may think that I should have put this action first, because after all how can you spend time with God if you have a wedge. The fact is most of us are so busy we don't even realize there is a wedge. I want to share a beautiful true story about a precious soul who carried a wedge for years between herself and God and never knew it until this one day.

I have worked at numerous companies in my HR career and in multiple States and I recall how one day an employee came in to talk with me privately. She was an excellent employee, very dedicated and a very good at her job. At her desk you would find a collection of angels and she would often wear Angel pins, and clothes that would have angels in the print. There was no way you couldn't guess that she loved angels unless you were blind. Anyway, she came into my office and shut the door and looked up to me very seriously. Theresa, I want you to pray over me; the doctor told me that I have a tumor in my uterus the size of a grapefruit and that I have to have radiation treatments. I told her that I in fact knew of a Pastor who had the gift of healing and would call and arrange for him to pray over her; I promised that I would go with her. She said, no, I want you to pray over me. First of all, it is not a practice of mine to talk about God in my capacity as a Human Resources Director, but I would in some cases, recommend to an employee to seek spiritual counsel depending on what they are troubled by in their life circumstances. This was the first time anyone had ever asked me to pray over them for healing. It is not common and I don't even know if it would be considered an acceptable practice for a lay person in the Catholic Church to lay hands on a person, without direct permission, and pray for healing. Anyway, time was of an essence and I am a person who acts first and asks for forgiveness later. So, after work, I drove her to the holiest place I knew, the Blessed Sacrament Chapel, at the Parish I attended, and all of a sudden the Lord pressed on me a thought. Without even fully considering the complete meaning of the thought I shared with her: God is laying on my heart that it is time to remove the wedge between Himself and you before we pray for healing. He said all of the angels you have around you, have actually served as a barrier between Him and you. Does this mean anything to you? And in an instant she was weeping like a baby, she said that when she was 13 years old she was molested by her Baptist Minister and she never understood how God could have allowed such a terrible thing to happen to her. I was crying with her and conveyed to her how devastated God was that day that a person who was to be His special agent of grace and healing, chose to violate her in this way. This abuse is abominable to God! And God has always been close and has seen all of the good she had done throughout her life to help those less fortunate. She told me how she had never gone to Church since that day! After a big hugging and crying session, I prayed for her healing. And the next morning she went for her first radiation treatment after which they took another x-ray. The second x-ray showed no tumor; the doctor ordered another xray. That x-ray also showed no tumor! More importantly God showed to me that healing is mind, body and soul; and the importance of removing the wedges, the residual scar tissue that is standing in the way of a free-flowing Love between your soul and Him.

Some common Wedges between God and Souls:

Doubt and Unbelief is the greatest deterrent to having a close walk with God
Distractions and Time Management— I just fly by the seat of my pants
Lack of personal discipline— Bad Habits— Strongholds
Guilt, Don't want to appear to be a hypocrite
Don't go to Church; haven't been to Church in so long, I am afraid to go
I have done too many horrible things in my life; I am not worthy.
I don't believe that your works matter; it is Jesus' sacrifice on the cross that brings us our reward
I am divorced and I caused it through adultery.
I have never been a religious person
My current lifestyle I know is unacceptable to God and I don't know how to change
I have never been baptized
My heart is so broken I find it hard to believe God really cares about me
I was abused as a child and I cried out to God for help but He didn't come and rescue me.

Though I cannot be with you in your physical space, I firmly believe that in God there is no Time or Space and so I ask you to consider any wedges between yourself and God. Most wedges are created due to an experience such as that in the story above, where some trauma occurred in your life that you believe God should have protected you and so you just stopped believing in Him or stayed mad at Him. Perhaps you were close to God, came to know and understand His highest desires for you and chose to abandon this path and have lived a life separated from God, at a distance; not in communication with Him. Perhaps you weren't raised in a family that went to Church or had God as a part of Life, so the distance you feel is not guilt or shame but more like a NO FEELING. Sort of like how do you explain the taste of a lemon to someone who has never tasted a lemon or the color blue to a blind person. There are a number of wedges but all wedges are just as easy to remove for you as the one in the heart of my friend and colleague. I am going to pray for you right now.

Father God, You know all of the particular circumstances of this soul who is seeking to restore a perfect union, soul to soul, with you in their life. I ask you to shower upon them this moment a sense of your abiding JOY at the reunion with this precious soul. I ask you to send to them or inspire them to reach out to individuals who live lives soul to soul close to You to support them in their desire to enjoy more of this Heaven on Earth You are ushering into our World! I love you God my Creator and greatest lover of souls! Amen.

To my fellow Catholics do not deny yourself one more week of the tremendous graces of the Sacrament of Reconciliation; given our background and understanding, just avoiding Confession can create an unnecessary wedge of stubborn Pride and even allow a spirit of rebellion to set into our souls. This kind of wedge steals our JOY and takes away from our full enjoyment of the presence of God.

The third action is to Study. You must take charge of your own **Spirit**ual Development; you must build into your day at least 20 minutes of reading or listening to audio CDs by reputable Teachers. I strongly recommend that you start by asking your Priest or Pastor, Rabbi or Imam, or Spiritual Director for suggested readings. If you are not currently attending Church but were raised in a certain Church, start by going back there; I firmly believe that God put the specific portals to Him in our lives for a reason. If you have never been affiliated with a Church ask God to lead you; He will. I even recommend that you turn on the Television to the many religious programs that are on today; and pay attention to your inner stirrings. You will find a portal that will lead you to a community of people who are seeking to walk with God. If you have a foundational relationship with God and want to take it to the next level I recommend that you listen to presentations on God by Pastors and Teachers of other religions and denominations than your current denomination. Why? Because together we have a fuller picture of God; we can gain a more complete insight into our souls and how to develop our souls.

In summary, if you want to enjoy a Heaven on Earth existence you must learn to operate more and more from your SOUL, your center of Excellence.

You know you are operating from your Soul when it seems there is an everlasting fountain of pure JOY flowing inside. You know you are operating from the Soul when you see the beauty, first in everyone and everything. You know you are operating from your Soul when you lose yourself in the work and never seem to run out of solutions when you run into obstacles. You know you are operating from your Soul when you no longer get upset about things that won't matter in 10 seconds, 10 minutes or in 10 years! You know that you are operating from Your Soul, your center of Excellence, when you walk in deep Peace. When you are operating from Your Soul you are not: led around by your appetites for food, sex, and or power.

This is just a beginning but it should give you a place to start from; a bit of a standard to work with. The bottom line is, when you are operating from your soul, that part of you that lives on beyond your flesh, you have joy in adversity and creative energy in the midst of darkness.

HEAVEN on EARTH
Transformation Mission

I know most people think that I have gone off the deep end with this idea; but if that is so, leave me there! I completely believe with every cell in my body that we are to enjoy a taste of Heaven every step of our journey until we are swimming in Heavenliness across the bridge to the other side... across the thin veil that separates us from Heaven. You do understand the existence of the thin veil? Think about your spirit, how far would you say is the distance between your body and your spirit? The problem today is that we have so emulated our bodies, which indeed are extraordinarily designed, but we have yet to begin to understand the true nature and power of our souls/spirit.

Look around, you can't tell me you haven't noticed all of the movies and books being written and internet webinar series on THE SECRET and meditation? Anytime someone is talking or writing about the part of us that has no end, they are really talking about the SOUL. If you have studied and read the words of the greatest inventors of our day, you will also learn that they describe the moment of discovery as an experience of entering with their mind into this high vibrational space of themselves, where the whole idea manifested, and that missing bit of knowledge manifested

Get Crowned!

and they were able to make their thought/idea work in time and space. I believe these individuals have pressed in beyond the powers of their finite self and pierced the thin veil to the soul/mind and are describing how THE SOUL/Spirit/Mind faculties are used to bridge the gap between human thoughts/ideas and tangible manifestation. Michelangelo, if you have studied (go online and do so if you haven't) demonstrated his ability to do this in his art and in his drawings of an idea for a flying vehicle in the 1400's.

This heightened interest in teaching, coaching and mastering this process of creation/invention also prove true that it is inevitable that more breakthroughs are on the way….. These breakthroughs are spirit driven and the Vision I believe God has opened my heart and mind and spirit to comprehend is about our choice in the direction of our progression, toward destruction or toward HEAVEN. Obviously I am assuming that you share God's desire for us to uncover/fully master this highest design aspect of our humanity, your Soul, and progress toward Heaven. This progression toward Heaven, I have named, The Heaven on Earth by the end of this decade project.

So to begin with let us paint a picture of Heaven, and you must understand, given its revolutionary concept, it will be a painting that will paint itself gradually and ever more completely with time. It is a concept that allows room for every soul to paint his or her own version; the very painting of it will reveal to you your own spiritual development, your own Heaven-readiness. Do not worry, even if you are Heaven-ready it doesn't mean that you will be leaving the Earth anytime soon; on the contrary, the Kingdom building all around you, your assignment(s) will become crystal clear and energizing like never before!

Heaven, what will it be like? Here are a few thoughts and I will have an email address where I would love to have your thoughts on it...together I believe we could paint a most extraordinary painting.

1) I imagine when I get to Heaven, everyone will love me; their eyes will light up when they see me.
2) In Heaven I never have to concern myself with how I look, or check the color of my skin before I engage someone; I will know with every ounce in my being, without a shadow of doubt that I was beautifully, wonderfully made!
3) In Heaven I will never fear rejection; I will be surrounded by a complete sensibility of inclusion, an unlimited space for everyone's greatness to exist in a perfectly symphonic way!
4) In Heaven I can love deeply, without fear of crossing boundaries, finally be allowed to eat, drink, dance, sing and just enjoy the amazingness of any and every soul in the universe!
5) In Heaven, no one will question the quality of my love, the purity of my heart's intention.
6) In Heaven, spontaneity will be celebrated and I will never see another sad and lonely, disappointed and dejected soul again.
7) In Heaven we will meet for the first time and we will see all that is good, all that is beautiful, all that is unique, all that is incredible about one another, and know each other as if for an eternity.

Seven is a number of fullness and so I will stop here... and I can feel a bedside meditation book being born.... And I weep with JOY at just these 7 snapshots. These snapshots make me excited about entering the fullness of Heaven one day and I cannot wait to hear yours! *So let me take it to the next step:*

Since God has revealed to me that He wants us to get ON ASSIGNMENT, "Thy Kingdom come, Thy Will be done, on Earth as it is in Heaven, I came to understand, through a "begin with the end in mind" strategy the following next step. Imagine how the Earth would be impacted if we, all of us, one by one, began to implement these qualities of Heaven into our earthly lives. What would the experience of our life be like, and how would these little changes transform our relationships, our families, our businesses, our schools, our communities, our Churches, our cities, our country, the World?

1. I imagine when I get to Heaven, everyone will love me; their eyes will light up when they see me.

From this moment going forward, we practice consciously to smile with our eyes and enthusiastically greet everyone we meet. I know, some of you are exhausted just thinking about being that in tune with your connections to others.... You just want to get down to business or get on with the day at hand. I promise, if you just incorporate this one practice, you will transform your life overnight, inside out.

Maya Angelou, on an Oprah Show I watched, once said that the greatest gift a parent could give to their child is that every time he or she came into your company/presence, your face lit up! We have gotten so busy that we have neglected the most important aspect of our relationships with one another, the quality of our connections and intersections throughout the day.

Heaven on Earth Challenge

Take charge of the quality of your connection and intersection with others today; look up from your computer, your book or IPad, newspaper, TV or cell phone, and honor the person who is talking to you with an eye to eye, heart/mind/soul present connection. Smile at everyone.

2. In Heaven I never have to concern myself with how I look, or check the color of my skin before I engage someone; I will know with every ounce in my being, without a shadow of doubt that I was beautifully, wonderfully made!

I cannot tell you how many people I have met who are waiting to do their highest life until they achieve a certain weight, or avoid their true callings because they don't fit the mold! And I can't wait for the day where the color of our skin just never enters into the equation. The beautifully wonderfully made is not focused on the body only, it is our whole unique person. I actually had a Prophet once say to me, until you know who you are before God, you will never touch the world on the level God has in mind for you. This prophecy was very distasteful to me at the moment, but over time I realized that I had accepted an invisible backseat position after I left the convent. Imagine if Paul Allen or Bill Gates had waited until they believed their idea would work; we might not have the Personal Computers today.

Heaven on Earth Challenge

What have you held back on in your life? Have you allowed the color of your skin or of another stop you from having a connection? Look in the mirror and tell yourself, I am beautifully and wonderfully made after every shower and think it in your mind as you interface with people all day long.... Even the person who cuts you off on the highway!

3. In Heaven I will never fear rejection; I will be surrounded by a complete sensibility of inclusion an unlimited space for everyone's greatness to exist in a perfectly symphonic way!

Fear of rejection is the number one reason individuals give for not doing what is truly on their heart to do; in Heaven this is not going to exist at all! I propose that if we begin to create around us a vibrant sense of inclusion, welcome, and invite the contribution and ideas of others into our daily life interfaces, I believe we will be creating a space in the universe where Fear of Rejection cannot exist…a little more Heaven on Earth. I just learned that scientists have discovered that if our bodies have a certain Ph balance, cancer and disease cannot exist. Note, this idea crosses over the religious thought of the vast majority of our world; this is why I am convinced it is a GOD thing!

Heaven on Earth Challenge

Today create a warm, welcoming and "We Need Your Greatness Too!", atmosphere and watch genius show up and breakthrough results abound. The latest highly successful business model is a collaboration of like-minded, highly talented people promoting and prospering from each other's contribution.

4. In Heaven I can love deeply, without fear of crossing boundaries, and finally be allowed to eat, drink, dance, sing and just enjoy the amazingness of any and every soul in the universe!

This is one of my greatest longings; one that has caused me more pain in this journey than any other. You see as a nun, I never had to worry about being propositioned for sex! I enjoyed meeting 1,000's of people, and was trusted with heart and soul intimacies, without worrying about someone thinking "something was going on". Since leaving the convent, it has been like a landmine avoidance expedition. Since there has been so much brokenness and betrayal of trust and continuous stimulation of the sexual side of our humanity, we have been cut off from a very important supply of positively nurturing energy from each other. Remember, I met souls that I often never met again, so I learned how to make deep connections, think of Jesus, now, so as to be able to touch their soul in a way that would encourage them to choose their best life!

On this attribute, I must take a little more time. In this day and age, it seems commonly accepted that if you deeply love someone it is just natural to express your love sexually; after all, it isn't every day that we love this deeply. I have come to understand that in fact, we were made to connect this deeply with everyone, this deep loving connection is a taste of Heaven, and it will be shared between all souls automatically, without effort in Heaven. So, instead of thinking that you found THE ONE, understand that you just finally broke through and experienced Love on its highest level. It might be THE ONE, but judging the divorce rate statistics, it was more often not THE ONE. In fact I would go so far as to say that you should come to love many this deeply first, without sex, as that is to be exchanged with THE ONE only, because of its super glue bonding properties. This original design of God for human beings has been distorted in a million ways and has now got us more tied in knots and separated from one another than ever. If we would remove this "sexual presumption" and keep it in its proper place, we could be enjoying an amazing flow of LOVING and SUPPORTIVE energy across all souls that could remove the peak level of sadness and aloneness everywhere today. I hardly meet happily married couples; this is a crying shame. Marriage and Family should be Heaven on Earth but this cannot happen in a vacuum!

Heaven on Earth Challenge

Look at your marriage and family is everyone growing, smiling, and using their gifts and talents? With The Crown in mind, do your part to encourage all to be using their gifts and talents, not burying them. Incorporate a Dinner Party or BBQ into your plans in the next 30 days and do so quarterly. Your Home should most resemble Heaven; where a continuous flow of interesting people come and go!

5. In Heaven, everything is easy and I will not be separated from those I love by time and distance.

I am most excited about this reality and looking back over the last 50 – 100 years, it is so clear that we are already moving rapidly toward Heaven in this area. So much of what we do today to live and enjoy life has become easier through technological advancements which translates to mean that some individual, pressing in with their intellectual powers with the faculties of their soul, until they come up with an easier way. By the end of this 2020 decade, I believe that we will see advancements that have not yet been conceived!

I am amazed that through SKYPE and the internet the separation from those I love has been diminished exponentially. I am currently studying Astral Projection so that I can actually travel by Spirit and be with those I love in their physical space.

Heaven on Earth Challenge

Look around and appreciate how much easier your life is compared to previous generations and ask yourself how are you exercising your soul power to enjoy a deeper Heaven-like union with those you love on this side and the next? Allow this reflection to convince you of the TRUTH of this Heaven on Earth progression!

6. In Heaven, spontaneity will be celebrated and I will never see another sad and lonely, disappointed and dejected soul again.

Spontaneity is "Live Creation" and it seems that most have lost this wonderful ability. It is the greatest secret to a youthful spirit and continuous high energy.

It is so troubling for me the number of faces I see that look sad, lonely, angry, disappointed, burdened and dejected by Life. This points so much to our disconnection from one another. I am not speaking of the moments of disappointment or a period of sadness after the death of a loved one; I am referring to the sadness that sets in when individuals stop reaching out to connect with others.

I imagine that it will take us all eternity to meet everyone in Heaven, so these skills of striking up a conversation with complete strangers will prepare us for Heaven! You will be amazed; people like to talk about themselves and rarely does anyone just spontaneously engage them in a conversation; even in marriages and families.

The Heaven on Earth Challenge

Today, engage someone in a conversation just to find out their story. Be open to telling your story, too; you never know how this exchange could encourage and enlighten you. We are in this journey together, now and for all eternity; let's stop walking like strangers next to one another. Can you see how Heaven is a coming?

7. In Heaven we will meet for the first time and we will see all that is good, all that is beautiful, all that is unique, all that is incredible about one another, and know each other as if for an eternity.

I imagine that by the end of this decade I will have created such a Heaven on Earth move, or rather so many souls would be attracted to participate in this Project that I will begin to experience this taste of Heaven more and more and more. I will find myself meeting individuals who have read my book and participated in developing a Crown-based business and when we meet finally face to face at a Conference; it will be like we have known each other forever.

We will already enjoy a connection on the soul level because of our shared interest in the Heaven on Earth Transformation Project. It will be completely JOY-FILLED and energizing to share their company and time will fly by!

Heaven on Earth Challenge

It is so easy to get "used to" those individuals we are married to, work with, go to Church with or with whom we have been friends a long time. It is also pretty easy to fall into the habit of collecting the long list of negatives. Today, write a list of everything you think is beautiful, unique, incredible about your spouse, buy a card and write it to them. Can you see Heaven coming to the Earth, now?

Living with THE CROWN in mind

7 Simple Ideas to keep THE CROWN
in the forefront of your mind

1) Put a picture of a CROWN on your mirror.
2) Join my email list and I will send you special reflections.
3) Buy a crown and lay it on top of your spiritual reading on your bedside.
4) Put into your schedule, first thing in the morning, at midday, and at the end of your day, time to connect with God, time to just sit in His presence and enjoy the thoughts of His gaze smiling upon you simply because you chose to spend time with Him.
5) Chose a relationship you are going to focus upon, that you know you have neglected for quite some time and invest special quality time nurturing it back to a worthy of a gem crown relationship.
6) Chose a particular gem you would really like God to reward you with: integrity, chastity, fidelity, honesty, dependability, loving, generous… and then write that character trait every time you doodle or take notes or journal.

7) Practice Forgiveness; review your heart to see if you are holding anyone in unforgiveness and release them and be slow to anger and quick to forgive today.

CROWN-based Communities

To those of you who may be interested in being a part of developing a special Event program designed to organize community partners around local schools, please let me know. We are believing that we can do more good if we work together and build a network of partners that can help to spread this message of bringing the SOUL to the work we are doing, We have lived in a time in our country where God has been systematically removed from the schools and any public agency. As a result, the highest part of our humanity, the soul has also been essentially banned from any forum except in the Church setting or certain very small-prescribed pockets.

This has hurt us as a nation and has given the next generation the message that God and the soul are not important to Life, and that God and the Soul are not worthy of being included in Education or Government. This is the wrong message. I hope this book has inspired you to join me in finding clever ways to incorporate The Crown into programs so as to orient our youth, our families, our colleagues and our neighbors that we are all going to one day stand before God, our creator and give an accounting of our lives.

CROWN-based Business Partners

This book is just the beginning of this campaign. It is in my plan to develop every dimension of the businesses that follow with The Crown in mind. Along the lines of my reflection on Heaven, I believe that it is possible to design highly profitable businesses by highlighting and promoting the skills and expertise of all partners. I would love to have your business featured on my website and will be looking to partner in the future with various types of businesses. If you would be interested in being a part of designing a template CROWN-based business start-up kit that will be offered for sale, and or would be interested in a co-promotional business relationship, just email me at: GetCrowned2@gmail.com

Some business activities we foresee participating in:

GET CROWNED VBS program
Heaven On Earth Transformation Project
THE CROWN jewelry and clothing line

Final Thoughts

It is in my heart to create a global marketing campaign that would put THE CROWN symbol everywhere to remind us of our common destiny. One day, one moment in time we shall all, one by one, meet our Creator and give an accounting of our lives. I know that we may, by our differing understanding of God, carry a deeply embedded belief about how it will take place; I hope that I was able to convey what I believe to be His Heart, and how He so longs for you to understand and believe this message. He loves you so much and He has loved you from the moment He conceived you in His thought and He so longs that you would discover the height, and breadth, and depth of His design of you, your greatness, mind, body and SOUL. He wants to reassure you that the Earth is not on the brink of destruction but on the verge of a breakthrough to an ERA of innovation arrived at through the highest component of his design of us, our soul.

A couple of years ago, I was preparing for a Sunday School Faith formation class for youth, 10 – 14, and as an opening I asked them, are you the generation? Are you the generation who will actually bring Thy Kingdom come, Thy Will be done, on Earth as it is in Heaven, into reality? The Our Father prayer is prayed across all Christian denominations, and at every AA and recovery meeting, and

I told them that I believed that I had prayed it at least 25,000 times in my life, and that I was tired of waiting for it to show up!!! I looked straight into their sweet eyes and asked them, "are you the generation, the Heaven on Earth generation?" You could hear a pin drop and all of their eyes were glued on every word I said. And so I ask of you, every morning I look in the mirror and ask myself, are you the generation, who before leaving this planet, will make it more like Heaven?

I hope you recognize, I didn't ask you to leave your Church, your family, your job, your homeland; nor did I require you to join a Church….. it requires a few shifts of your perspective and a commitment to live your highest life in the 24/7 not just at Church.

I am also inviting you to join us in creating a virtual Crown-based community so as to provide opportunities to work collaboratively, stay focused and committed together, and create mastermind groups that will support the realization of this Heaven on Earth era… … one soul at a time, one collaboration at a time! I so look forward to hearing from you soon! See you at **www.HeavenonEarthTransformation.com**.

Love,

Theresa Jordan

GET CROWNED!

www.ingramcontent.com/pod-product-compliance
Lightning Source LLC
Chambersburg PA
CBHW021430070526
44577CB00001B/149